The
Brown County
Cookbook

THE
BROWN COUNTY
COOKBOOK

Nancy C. Ralston
and
Marynor Jordan

Illustrated by Nancy C. Ralston

INDIANA UNIVERSITY PRESS
Bloomington

Manufactured in the United States of America

Library of Congress Cataloging in Publication Data

Ralston, Nancy C.
The Brown County cookbook.

Includes index.
1. Cookery, American — Indiana. 2. Brown county (Ind.)
— Social life and customs. I. Jordan, Marynor.
II. Title.
TX715.R158   1983   641.5   83 – 47917
ISBN 0 – 253 – 21250 – 2 (pbk.)
1 2 3 4 5 87 86 85 84 83

To Bonnie B. Irvin, who continues to cherish Hoosier home cooking and the Indiana countryside after more than ninety years.

Indiana,
the home of art and letters
and of old-fashioned cookery,
is as noble a slice of earthy cake
as this country can show.

Irvin S. Cobb
1924

Acknowledgments

Archives of the Brown County Historical Society

Kin Hubbard,
Abe Martin's Almanack,
Abe Martin Publishing Co.,
Indianapolis, 1908

Management of:
Abe Martin Lodge
Carrousel's Brown County Inn
Brown County Ramada Inn and Convention Center
Nashville House
The Ordinary

The old, two-leaf table can scarcely stand under the weight of dark colored preserves in heavy glass dishes of primitive design. The same big blue tureen is on the board filled with mashed potatoes. The castor and the bone-handled butter knife — every familiar object, everything you used to like, is there. You are eating at home again.

Abe Martin's Brown County Almanack
1908

Contents

Brown County, Indiana

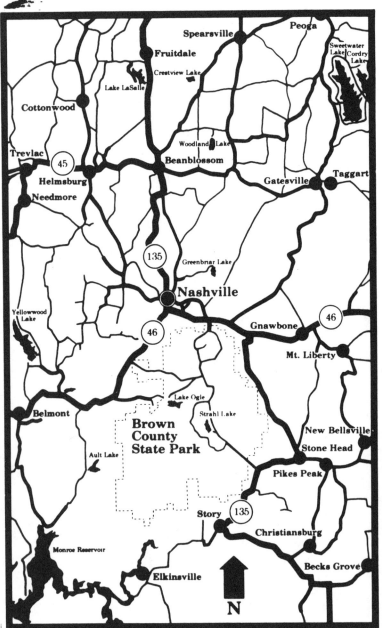

Peoga

Spearsville

Fruitdale

Sweetwater Lake | Cordry Lake

Crestview Lake

Lake LaSalle

Cottonwood

Woodland Lake

Trevlac

Beanblossom

45

Gatesville

Taggart

Helmsburg

Needmore

135

Greenbriar Lake

Nashville

Yellowwood Lake

46

Gnawbone

46

Mt. Liberty

Lake Ogle

Belmont

Strahl Lake

Brown County State Park

New Bellsville

Stone Head

Ault Lake

Pikes Peak

Monroe Reservoir

Story

135

Christiansburg

Becks Grove

Elkinsville

N

Andy Rogers, Nashville, Indiana

INTRODUCTION

ABE MARTIN! – dad-burn
his old picture!
P'tends he's a
Brown county fixture –

James Whitcomb Riley

What's Cookin' in Brown County?

Early Brown County settlers, much like the Indians who preceded them, enjoyed an abundance of wild game and vegetation. Among the meats which came to the tables in those pioneer homes were venison, possum, squirrel, rabbit, raccoon, wild hogs, and muskrat. Quail, duck, pheasant, pigeon, and wild turkey, as well as fresh fish allowed newcomers to the territory to feast on a variety of dishes.

Wild fruit, including berries, grapes, persimmons, paw paws, and crab apples, provided the makings for the puddings, pies, and cakes which, along with homemade sorghum molasses, maple syrup and honey, helped to satisfy many a sweet tooth. Dandelion greens, poke sprouts, wild asparagus, and mushrooms supplemented the vegetables cultivated in every garden. Much "butcherin' " and "puttin' up" home-grown produce were necessary to keep larders well supplied.

In 1905, at a time when Brown County probably was still the poorest and the most inaccessible area in the entire state of Indiana, Kin Hubbard's legendary cartoon character Abe Martin said from the pages of the *Indianapolis News,* "By crackey, it's sum travelin ter git ter Brown County." Later, Kin Hubbard became a famous syndicated columnist for over 25 years and his rustic Brown County philosopher was a national favorite, helping to bring additional attention and fame to the art colony forming in the "hills o' Brown." In 1932, the lodge constructed in the middle of 13,000-acre Brown County State Park was dedicated to Abe Martin, and surrounding cabins were named after some of his Brown County friends and neighbors. A glassed-in wall display of Kin Hubbard's many Abe Martin books can be found outside of the dining room at the Nashville House.

Many years have passed since Kin Hubbard described the area as "a county whose natives for the most part subsist by blackberrying, sassafras-mining and basket weaving." Some things, to be sure, have changed. Accessibility, for instance, improved greatly when state highways connected the county seat of Nashville with Indianapolis, Bloomington, and Columbus. Today, during the peak of the autumn tourist season, everyone, including out-of-state visitors, would seem to travel each of the routes to Nashville all at the same time.

Sassafras tea still is available in local restaurants and blackberrying remains a seasonal pastime, however basket weavers have been joined by artisans and craftsmen of every description. The sheriff's log in the weekly newspaper continues to report dog fights and lost cattle and Abe Martin, were he still around, would find that many things about Brown County never change, especially the beauty of its hazy landscape. Far from the crowded streets of Nashville, snug cabins and rambling farm houses continue to dot the colorful hills, and in many of these remote kitchens, country cooking is still in style. Family recipes are handed down from one generation to another. Those selected for this book were gathered in all corners of the county from "Peogie" to Beck's Grove and Gnaw Bone to Needmore. "A pinch of this," "a handful of that," and "it don't make any difference how big your hand is" have been changed into recognizable units of measurement. Any variation from an original has been treated with great care lest anything be lost in translation. Some of the same "vittles" that satisfied the hearty appetites of early Brown County settlers go right on pleasing more recent emigrants and other "furriners" who like to sample some of the joys of a more simple life.

This book allows the city dweller to prepare country fare. Ingredients in the majority of recipes are found in most markets. In a separate section, "Something Wild in the Kitchen," wild or indigenous items are included for the forager or adventurer who has the time and desire to try examples of what could, in time, become the lost art of true country cooking.

Some of Kin Hubbard's remarks and Abe Martin's sayings about cooking and eating are included for a true taste of cracker-barrel philosophy. The reader is invited to savor each one.

Nancy C. Ralston
Marynor Jordan

OF THE GRAINS
Breads, Biscuits, Fritters, Pancakes

A husband will often say things in a burst o' hunger that he fully regrets after he has bought his breakfast downtown.

Baking Powder Biscuits

2 c. flour
1 t. salt
1 c. milk
4 t. baking powder
4 T. shortening

Sift together, dry ingredients, work in shortening, stir in liquid gradually, and roll on floured board to 1-in. thickness. Cut with biscuit cutter or edge of drinking glass. Bake at 400 degrees until browned.

A young wife's biscuits make a dandy border for a geranium bed.

Cheese Biscuits

2 c. flour
3 t. baking powder
3 T. lard
1/4 t. salt
1/2 c. cheese, grated
1 c. milk

Sift together flour and baking powder. Work in lard, salt, cheese, and milk. Make a soft dough and pat out on floured board to about 1-in. thick. Cut small biscuits and bake 10 or 12 min. in medium hot oven.

Fried Biscuits (Nashville House)

2 2/3 pkg. dry yeast or 1/6 c. yeast
1 qt. milk
1/4 c. sugar
1/2 c. lard or shortening
6 t. salt
7 to 9 c. flour

Add yeast to warm water. Add other ingredients and let dough rise. Work into biscuits and drop into hot fat.

Biscuits and Gravy

4 T. pork sausage drippings
3 T. flour
milk or water
salt and pepper
hot biscuits

Blend flour into drippings. Stir until smooth. Cook slowly while adding milk or water, until gravy has pleasing thickness. Season with salt and pepper. Serve over hot biscuits. Makes about 2 c.

Brown Bread

1 c. cornmeal
1 c. graham flour
1 c. rye flour
1 t. salt
2 t. soda
1 c. sorghum
1 c. sweet milk
1/2 c. sour milk

Mix ingredients until smooth. Steam in 1-lb. cans with a tight lid for 3 hours. Remove from cans. Bake 10 min. at 400 degrees.

Soft Cornbread

1 pt. milk
1/2 pt. cornmeal.
1/2 t. salt
2 T. butter
3 eggs, separated and beaten

Heat half the milk, stir the other half into the cornmeal, add to the hot milk, cook until like mush, and add salt and butter. Add beaten yolks to mixture and then the whites. Bake 20 min. in moderate oven. Serve immediately.

Flannel Cakes

1 c. flour
1/4 t. salt
1 t. baking powder
3/4 c. milk
1/2 T. butter, melted
1 egg, separated and beaten

Mix dry ingredients, add milk and melted butter to yolk of egg. Mix all together. When a smooth batter has been made, beat well, then fold in stiffly beaten egg white. Bake on hot griddle.

A cold pancake is a total loss.

Potato Pancakes

2 c. stiff mashed potatoes
1 egg
1 T. onion, chopped
flour
butter

Stir egg and onion into mashed potatoes. Form patties and dredge in flour. Fry in butter until golden brown.

Popovers

2 c. milk
2 eggs
2 heaping T. butter, melted
pinch of salt
2 heaping t. baking powder
flour

Beat milk, eggs, butter, and salt. Add baking powder and enough flour to make medium thick batter. Bake in greased gem pans 50 min. at 375 degrees.

Spoon Bread

1 c. white cornmeal
1 1/2 c. boiling water
2 eggs, separated
1 c. milk
1 t. salt
2 t. baking powder

Mix cornmeal and boiling water; cool to lukewarm. Add yolks of eggs, well-beaten, with milk, salt, and baking powder. Fold in stiffly beaten egg whites. Bake in greased 2-qt. baking dish at 325 degrees for about 1 hr.

Cornmeal Griddle Cakes

1 c. boiling water
3/4 c. yellow cornmeal
1 T. sorghum
1 c. sour milk
2 eggs
1 1/2 t. salt
3 t. baking powder
1/4 t. soda
1 1/2 c. flour
3 T. shortening, melted
1/2 to 3/4 c. nuts, broken

Pour water over cornmeal and stir until thick, add sorghum and milk. Beat in eggs. Sift salt, baking powder, and soda with flour. Add to mixture and stir in shortening. Pour on a hot ungreased griddle. Sprinkle nuts over each cake at once. Makes about 30 3-in. pancakes.

Corn Fritters

1 3/4 c. all-purpose flour
2 t. baking powder
3/4 t. salt
2 T. sugar
1 c. milk or juice from canned corn or both
1 egg, slightly beaten
1 c. canned corn, drained
1 T. fat, melted

Sift first 4 ingredients together. Mix liquid, egg, and corn. Gradually add this mixture to dry ingredients. Add the melted fat. Soaked, dried corn, cooked until tender, may be used. Drop batter by spoonfuls into hot fat. Drain and serve hot with syrup. Good with ham, fried chicken, or pork.

Cheese and Rice Fritters

1 c. boiled rice
1/2 c. cheese, grated
2 T. milk or butter, melted
1 egg
2 t. flour
1 t. baking powder
1/2 t. salt.

Mix ingredients. Drop by spoonfuls on well-greased griddle. Use medium low heat. Fry until golden brown on both sides.

Cornmeal Mush

1 c. cornmeal
4 c. water
1 t. salt

Mix cornmeal with 1 c. water. Bring to a boil 3 c. water and the salt. Pour into cornmeal mixture. Stir until thick. Place on low heat 30 min., stir once in a while. For a thicker mush, use 2 c. water for every c. cornmeal.

Eat hot with butter, as a vegetable, or slice cold for frying and serve with butter and molasses.

Potato Rolls

1 c. warm potato water
1/2 c. sugar
1/2 cake compressed yeast
1 c. potatoes, mashed
1 c. shortening
4 eggs, well-beaten
1 t. salt
flour (enough to make soft dough)
butter, melted

Mix potato water, sugar, and yeast together early in the morning. Keep quite warm but not hot. Let stand until foamy and light. Add other ingredients. Let rise until light. Roll to about 1/2 in. Run over melted butter, fold over and cut with biscuit cutter. Place in buttered pans (not too close). Let rise until very light. Bake 20 minutes in moderate oven.

Potato Muffins

3/4 c. milk
1 c. cold mashed potatoes
1 1/2 c. flour
1/2 t. salt
4 t. baking powder
2 eggs, beaten
2 T. shortening, melted

Add milk to potatoes and mix well. Sift flour, salt, and baking powder. Mix with potatoes and milk, then add beaten eggs. If potatoes are very dry, add a little more milk. Add melted shortening last. Bake in greased muffin tins in moderate oven 30 min.

Gingerbread Waffles

2 c. flour
1 1/2 t. ginger
1/2 t. cinnamon
1/2 t. salt
1 c. molasses
1/3 c. butter
1 1/2 t. soda
1/2 c. sour milk
1 egg, beaten

Sift first 4 ingredients together. Next, heat molasses and butter to boiling point, but do not boil. Remove from stove and beat in soda, sour milk, egg, then sifted dry ingredients. Bake in waffle iron, watching carefully. Serve with whipped cream, sweetened and flavored to taste.

I would just as leave eat a padlock as a hand-me-down donut.

BIRD AND BEAST
Poultry and Meat

Nobuddy ever listened t' reason
on a' empty stomach.

Fricasseed Chicken and Dumplings

Dress the fowl and cut it into pieces for serving. Roll each piece in flour and brown in hot fat. Browning the chicken before cooking it helps retain and develop the flavor. After the pieces are browned, simmer, in enough water to cover, until tender. When it is done, take the chicken out and cook dumplings in the gravy. Serve the chicken in the center of a platter with the dumplings around the edge. Pour the gravy over the chicken.

Dumplings
1 c. flour
2½ t. baking powder
½ t. salt
1 egg
5½ T. milk

Sift flour, baking powder, and salt together. Beat the eggs well, add milk, and mix with dry ingredients. Drop by small spoonfuls into the chicken gravy. Cover tightly and cook 15 min. If steam escapes, dumplings will not be light.

Smothered Chicken

Cut up the chicken as for frying, season, dredge well with flour, put in skillet with about ½ c. butter and lard, and pour over it 1 c. of hot water. Cover tightly and bake in oven 1½ hr. When done take out the chicken and make a gravy in the skillet. This is a good way to cook chicken too old to fry.

Chicken Pie

Prepare chicken by stewing until tender and meat separates from the bone. Bone, leaving medium-sized pieces of chicken, and cut up with scissors some of the tender skin. Cook down the water the chicken was cooked in and make a thin gravy. Place chicken in casserole and cover with gravy. Use following for the crust:

2 c. flour
1 c. milk
2 t. baking powder
1 t. salt
1 egg, well-beaten
2 T. butter, melted

Work all to a smooth paste and drop by large spoonfuls on top of chicken and bake.

Roast Goose

Select a goose not too fat, rub inside thoroughly with salt, after having wiped dry inside and out. Rub outside with butter, then with flour. This makes a paste which keeps the goose moist. The dressing should not be very moist. For dressing use bread crumbs, sage, 1 small onion, 1 chopped apple, and 1/2 c. melted butter poured over the crumbs. Fill goose with stuffing, place breast up in roaster, and bake uncovered at 325 degrees until tender or 4 or 5 hrs. for a 10 to 12 lb. goose.

Lots of Christmases have been ruined by not carving the turkey in the kitchen.

Ham and Eggs

Fry ham slices in butter. Break eggs over top. Add 1 T. water. Cover skillet with lid and let steam until eggs are set. Lift out ham with eggs on top and serve.

Baked Ham

Place 2-in.-thick slice of ham in a large baking dish. Spread with brown sugar. Quarter 1 large cooking apple. Cut 1 orange into very thin slices. Place fruit around edge of ham. Pour, over all, 1 pt. canned tomatoes. Bake slowly in 350 – degree oven until ham is tender.

Smothered Ham and Sweet Potatoes

1 slice of smoked ham, cut into sizes for serving
3 c. raw sweet potatoes, sliced
2 T. sugar
1 c. hot water
1 T. ham drippings

Brown the ham lightly on both sides and arrange it to cover the bottom of a baking dish. Spread the sliced sweet potatoes over the ham. Sprinkle with sugar. Add the hot water and extra fat. Cover the dish and bake slowly until the ham is tender. Baste the potatoes occasionally with the gravy. Brown the top well.

Pressed Meat

2/3 lb. beef
1/3 lb. pork
salt and pepper

Boil until tender and grind through a food chopper. Make a thin gravy with stock and mix with meat. Season with salt and pepper. Pack into a loaf pan or mold. Cover with waxed paper and weight down with a heavy object. Slice when cool.

Pork Barbecue

Parboil slabs of pork ribs for 5 min. Drain and place on racks at least 5 in. above hot coals. Grill for 45 to 60 min. turning frequently, until tender. During the last 20 min. or so, baste with sauce.

Barbecue Sauce (Carrousel's Brown County Inn)
1 No. 10 can catsup
4 c. chili sauce
1 lb. brown sugar
1 T. Liquid Smoke
1/3 c. dry mustard
1/3 c. chili powder
1/3 c. Worcestershire sauce
1/3 c. white sugar

Combine ingredients and simmer about 20 min. Makes 5 qt.

Scrapple

Boil the head of a freshly slaughtered pig or use scraps and bones from pork roast and chops. Neckbones, feet, and knuckles are also good to use in this manner. Cook at least 3 lb. of boney pieces. For each lb. of bones use 1 qt. of water. Simmer until meat falls off bones. Drain meat and reserve liquid. Chop meat, removing all pieces of bone.

If reserved broth does not equal 2 qt., add water to make this quantity. Bring to a boil and add 2 c. cornmeal. Cook until mixture thickens, stirring constantly. Add chopped meat, salt, and other seasoning like sage and thyme. Pour into loaf pan and allow to cool. When firm, slice and brown in skillet. Slices may be dipped in egg and then flour and egg again, if crustier scrapple is preferred.

Meat and Potato Country Pie

In a greased baking dish put a thin layer of mashed potatoes, dressed with butter, milk, and salt. Next place a layer of chopped meat seasoned with salt, pepper, parsley, and a trace of onion, or a layer of well-seasoned, slightly thickened stew, creamed chicken, or creamed fish. There should be no potatoes in the stew. Top with another layer of mashed potatoes. Bake until the pie is hot and lightly browned on top. A small amount of baking powder or a well-beaten egg adds to the lightness of the potato.

A counter irritant is a feller that has jist paid fer a rib-roast.

Red Flannel Hash

2 c. leftover corned beef, chopped
2 c. beets, cooked and chopped
2 c. potatoes, cooked and diced
1 onion, chopped
butter or bacon drippings
Worcestershire sauce
salt and pepper

Combine all ingredients and mix well. Melt butter in large iron skillet. Add hash and cook until potatoes begin to brown.

Chicken-Fried Steak

1/2-in. thick round steak
flour
salt
shortening

Pound steak to tenderize. Dredge thinned meat in mixture of flour and salt. Melt shortening in large iron skillet. Quickly brown steak, turning once. Cut into portions and set aside. Make pan gravy from drippings.

Who remembers the old speckled oilcloth table cover full of slits where the knife glanced off the round steak?

Hoosier Flank Steak

Take a medium-sized flank steak, cut in finger-shaped pieces. Salt and pepper and dip in beaten egg and roll in cracker crumbs. Fry in hot fat, as you fry chicken using part butter. Place in roasting pan and cover with a quart of milk, bake slowly in medium oven for 1 hr., remove with spatula onto platter and make gravy as for chicken.

PUTTIN' UP
Jams, Jellies, Preserves, and Pickles

Who recalls the oldtime grocery store with everything uncovered and exposed and a big maltese cat asleep in the prunes?

Baked Apple Butter

3 lb. tart cooking apples, quartered
4 c. water
1 c. apple juice or cider
2 c. sugar
1 t. allspice, ground
2 t. cinnamon, ground
1 t. cloves, ground

Put quartered apples in large kettle, add water and cook until soft. Puree fruit by putting it through a sieve or food mill. Return to kettle, add other ingredients, bring to a boil and simmer, stirring frequently for 30 min. Pour into baking dish and bake in 300 – degree oven until thick. (Six or more hours). Pour into sterilized jars and seal. Makes about 2 pt.

Sweet Apple Pickles

1 lb. apples
1 c. vinegar
2 c. sugar
1/2 T. cinnamon, ground
speck ginger

Pare and core apples, drop into boiling syrup and cook tender. Place all in hot sterile jars.

Green Bean "Leather Britches"

Pick bush or pole beans at their peak. With a large needle, string beans about 1/2 in. apart on a clean string. Hang to dry near the ceiling over the cookstove. Before cooking, soak in cold water to restore. Cook in soaking water with appropriate seasonings.

Cabbage Relish

3 c. cabbage, shredded
2 c. onion, chopped
1 can pimento
3/4 c. sugar
salt and pepper to taste

Mix ingredients. Add enough very strong vinegar to dissolve sugar. Put in sealed jar and chill.

Green Cucumber Relish

To 1 large chopped cucumber add equal amount of chopped onion. To this add at least 1/2 teacup salt and mix thoroughly with a silver fork. Allow to stand overnight or 1/2 day until ready to drain. Season with whole mustard seed, black pepper, and cold cider vinegar sufficient to cover the dry ingredients. A little chopped green pepper is thought by some to be a good addition.

Pickled Eggs

2 doz. fresh eggs
6 c. vinegar
2 T. peppercorns
1 T. whole allspice
2 T. sugar
1/2 t. cloves
10 small red hot peppers

Boil eggs for 12 min. Place in cold water to cool immediately. Remove shells and pack eggs in sterilized jars. Bring remaining ingredients to a boil. Simmer for 5 min. and pour over eggs. Seal and store in cool, dark place.

Grape Butter

4 lb. Concord grapes
3 lb. sugar

Remove grape skins and set aside. Heat pulp for 15 min. Force pulp through sieve or food mill to remove seeds. Simmer skins, pulp, and sugar, stirring frequently, for 15 min. Makes about ten 8-oz. glasses.

Grape Catsup

Wash and stem 5 lb. grapes. Boil in a little water until soft. Strain through sieve. Add:

3 lb. sugar
1 pt. vinegar
1/2 T. salt
1 T. cloves, ground
1 T. cinnamon
1 T. pepper

Boil until thick. Bottle and seal.

Quince Honey

3 quinces
8 pears
4 lb. sugar
3 c. water

Peel and quarter fruit. Put through a food mill or meat grinder. Make a simple syrup by mixing sugar and water together and heating slowly to a boil. Add fruit and cook for 40 min. or longer. Pour into sterilized jars and seal.

> *Next to smelling a marigold nothing whizzes us back to our childhood days like biting into a quince.*

Sun Preserves

6 c. strawberries, washed
6 c. sugar

Combine berries and sugar and mix thoroughly. Let berries rest for 30 min. then bring to a boil in an enamel pan. Pour heated mixture into shallow platters and place in direct sun. Cover with glass or waxed paper to keep insects and dust from settling on preserves. Bring platters in at night and return to sun on daily basis until preserves are very thick and syrupy. Pour into sterilized jars and seal.

Peach Sunshine

1 c. peaches, chopped
1 c. sugar

Boil 15 min. Pour into sterilized jars and seal.

As soon as some folks recover from their anxiety over th' peach crop they begin t' worry about th' late p'taters.

Pepper Hash

2 doz. sweet green peppers
2 doz. sweet red peppers
2 large onions
1 1/2 pt. sugar
1 1/2 pt. vinegar

Chop vegetables together. Cover with boiling water, let stand 10 min. then drain. Add sugar and vinegar. Cover and boil 20 min. Seal in jars.

Rhubarb Conserve

4 c. rhubarb, cut fine
4 c. sugar
2 oranges, juice and grated rind
2 lemons, juice and grated rind
1/4 t. salt
1 c. blanched almonds cut in small pieces

Combine all the ingredients except the nuts. Heat the mixture slowly until the sugar is dissolved, then boil rapidly until it is clear. The cooking time depends on the tenderness of the rhubarb, but do not cook the conserve too long and lose the attractive pink color and fresh flavor. Add the nuts, stir well and let the mixture cool before pouring into hot, clean jelly glasses. If the conserve is put in hot, the nuts will rise to the top. This quantity will fill about 8 jelly glasses.

Nothing retards rhubarb, it could get out of a straight jacket.

Missionary Pickles

300 small cucumbers (size of middle finger)
1 gal. cider vinegar
1 c. sugar
1 c. salt
1 c. horseradish, ground
1 c. pickling spice
1/2 c. mustard, ground
1 piece of alum (size of end of thumb)

Scour cucumbers and place in a large stone crock. Add boiling water to cover. Let stand all night. Drain, combine remaining ingredients and pour over pickles. Place crock in a cool dark place. Allow pickles to sit for several days before using.

Watermelon Pickles

2 lb. watermelon
limewater made from 1 qt. water and 1 T. lime
4 c. vinegar
1 c. water
5 c. sugar
1 T. allspice
1 T. cloves
6 small pieces stick cinnamon

Pare and remove all green and pink portions from watermelon rind. Cut it to the desired shape or size and soak for 2½ hr. in the limewater. Drain the watermelon and place it in fresh water to cover, cook 1½ hr. or until tender. Let the watermelon stand overnight in the water. Make a syrup of the vinegar, water, sugar, and spices. Allow the syrup to come to the boiling point, add the drained watermelon and boil gently for 2 hr. or until the syrup is fairly thick. Seal and store. If desired, some of the pieces of the watermelon may be placed on waxed paper and allowed to dry out, turning every day or two until dry enough to store. This melon can be used in place of citron in cakes and puddings and may be dipped in chocolate or covered with fondant.

When the family sits down to canteloupe, they all ask at once, "Is yours good?"

37

Canned Sauerkraut

Cut cabbage on slaw cutter. Pack as tightly as possible in sterilized glass jars. Add 1 t. salt to each qt. jar. Fill with cold water and seal. Let stand in something to catch the drip and after 3 to 4 weeks it is ready to use.

Horseradish

Wash and scrape freshly dug horseradish. Tie dish towel over face and nose and then grind or grate roots. Sprinkle horseradish with salt, add white vinegar to cover. Pack in clean, dry jars and seal tightly.

SALADS OF ALL SORTS

*There's somebody at every
dinner party who eats celery.*

Cabbage Salad

1 large head fresh cabbage
2 large onions
3/4 c. sugar
1 t. celery seed
1 c. vinegar
1 t. salt
1/4 t. pepper
1 t. dry mustard
1 c. salad oil

Shred cabbage, slice onions and separate into rings. In a large bowl, layer cabbage and onions ending with onions on top. Combine remaining ingredients except for the oil. Bring mixture to a boil and remove from heat. Add oil, mix thoroughly and pour over vegetables. Do not stir. Cover salad and refrigerate for 24 hr.

Cabbage and Onion Salad

Shred the cabbage and cut onions into very thin rings. Season with salt, celery salt, pepper, and paprika. Mix with mayonnaise or French dressing and serve on a cabbage leaf.

Cole Slaw (Brown County Ramada Inn)

1 head cabbage, chopped
1/3 c. carrots, shredded
1 t. celery seed
1 t. salt
1 t. white pepper
1 1/2 t. sugar
2 1/2 c. salad dressing
1 t. herb blend (basil, thyme, marjoram, tarragon, fennel, celery, dill, and black pepper)

Combine ingredients, toss and chill.

Candle Salad

Place a whole slice of canned pineapple on a lettuce leaf. Stick ¹/₂ a banana upright in the center of the pineapple. Top the banana with a red cherry. Garnish with a yellow salad dressing to represent tallow running down the sides of a lighted candle.

Carrot and Apple Salad

1 carrot
1 apple
1 T. peanuts
pinch of salt
1 T. salad dressing or lemon juice

Grind carrot very fine. Grind apple very coarsely. Grind peanuts and mix. Serve on lettuce leaves.

*Th' hardest thing about gardenin' is t' keep
from raisin' too much lettuce.*

Fresh Green Pea Salad

1¹/₂ c. fresh peas, cooked
2 apples
1 c. celery
mayonnaise
lettuce
walnuts

Drain peas thoroughly. Dice apples and celery. Mix with the peas and pour on a boiled mayonnaise dressing. Arrange on lettuce leaves and garnish with walnuts. French dressing may be used if desired.

*The trouble with banquets is that they sit you so
close together it knocks the peas off your knife.*

Green Gage Salad

For a single serving. Three or 4 good sized cooked green gage plums and sufficient cream cheese to fill cavities after stones are removed. Serve on a lettuce leaf with mayonnaise dressing topped with whipped cream.

Melon Salad

2 envelopes gelatin
3 c. cantaloupe or honeydew, cubed
4 c. boiling water
juice of 2 lemons
1 c. sugar (scant)
food coloring, green or yellow

Dissolve gelatin in a little water. Add to fruit and pour in boiling water, lemon juice, sugar, and a little bit of food coloring. Ginger ale may be used in place of all water.

One good way to fix rutabaga is to pour kerosene on the roots.

Hoosier Salad (Carrousel's Brown County Inn)

8 carrots, sliced
4 green peppers, chunked
1 stalk celery, chunked
6 green onions, sliced
20 cherry tomatos, cut in half
4 cucumbers, 1/4-in. slices
1 c. salad oil
1/2 c. wine vinegar

Mix all ingredients, toss lightly and refrigerate until ready to serve. Add seasoning salt, if desired.

Spinach Salad (Carrousel's Brown County Inn)
Wash spinach. Dice green onions. Crumble cooked bacon.
Mix spinach, onions, bacon, and toss. Pour over dressing
and top with shredded hard boiled eggs.

Dressing
1/2 c. salad oil
1/2 c. sugar
1/4 c. catsup
2 T. Worcestershire sauce
1/4 c. wine vinegar
4 T. sunflower seeds
Heat all ingredients in saucepan until sugar melts, but
liquid does not boil. Cool, add sunflower seeds and stir.

I'll say this for spinach — it gives you lots o' grit.

Vegetable Salad
1 c. cabbage
1 c. carrots, cooked or raw, and chopped
1 c. beets, cooked and chopped
1 c. potatoes, cooked and chopped
1 c. celery, chopped
1 head lettuce, chopped
1 pimento, chopped
1 small onion, sliced
1 cucumber, sliced
1 bunch radishes, sliced
Mix all together, when ready. Serve with mayonnaise.

*If paper is made o' pulp it's funny the manufac-
turers hain't got on to the little red radishes
mother buys to brighten up the table.*

Stuffed Pepper Salad

Wash and remove the seeds from green peppers and drain thoroughly. Moisten cottage cheese with tomato sauce and fill peppers, packing the cheese in as solidly as possible. Put in a cold place at least 1 hr. Slice in ¼-in. slices. Arrange on lettuce and pour French dressing over it.

SOUPS AND STEWS

It's funny folks can't eat soup without thinking they're boiling out a cistern.

Broccoli and Cheese Soup (Abe Martin Lodge)

2 lb. broccoli, chopped
4 T. butter
4 T. flour
4 c. milk
1 t. salt
pinch of pepper
1/2 lb. American cheese

Cook broccoli until tender. Melt butter in saucepan; stir in flour. While stirring, add milk, salt, pepper, and cheese. Bring to a boil, add broccoli and let simmer 15 min. Serves 8.

Corn Chowder

2 T. salt pork, diced
1 onion, or more, if desired
1 qt. potatoes, diced
1 pt. boiling water
2 cups canned corn
1 pt. milk
salt and pepper

Cut the pork into small pieces and chop the onion. Boil the diced potatoes in the pt. of boiling water for 15 min. Fry the salt pork and onions for 2 min. and add these and the corn to the potatoes. Cook until the potatoes are done. Add the milk and season with salt and pepper. Bring the mixture to the boiling point. Serve very hot in soup dishes and place 2 or 3 crackers in the dish before pouring in the hot chowder.

Cream of Corn Soup

1 can corn, or 2 c. fresh corn
2 c. boiling water
1 t. salt
1/4 t. celery salt
3 T. butter, melted
2 1/2 T. flour
2 c. milk
1 c. cream, whipped

Rub corn through sieve, add the water, salt, and celery salt. Simmer slowly. Blend the melted butter, flour, and milk together carefully and cook 5 min. stirring constantly. Combine mixtures and just before serving add the cream.

Duck Soup

duck carcasses or other wild fowl
cold water
salt and pepper
1 large carrot, sliced
1 medium onion, chopped
2 stalks celery, diced
sugar

Place bones in large soup pot. Add water to cover. Simmer for several hours. Remove bones and set aside. Add vegetables and seasonings. Cook soup gently for 1 hr. or more. Scrape remaining meat from bones and add to soup. Correct seasoning.

Squash Soup

2 c. chicken or veal broth
1½ to 2 c. Hubbard or acorn squash, cooked and mashed
1 c. rich milk
1 t. salt
pepper
¼ t. onion juice
few drops lemon juice
parsley, chopped

Heat ingredients, except parsley, to boiling. Stir occasionally. Pour into bowls and sprinkle with parsley. Serve with French bread.

Quick Turnip Soup

4 cups milk
1 T. flour
2 T. butter
2 cups raw turnip, grated
½ t. onion, grated
1¼ t. salt
½ t. parsley, cut fine

Heat the milk in a double boiler, add flour and butter which have been well blended, then turnip, onion, and salt. Cook until turnip is tender, about 10 min. Sprinkle on parsley just before serving. Serve with croutons, if desired.

It is not proper to eat soup so you can notice it.

Potato Soup

4 medium-sized potatoes
1 medium-sized onion
1 t. salt
2 c. milk
3 T. butter
1 T. flour

Slice potatoes and onion, cover with 4 c. water and cook slowly until done. Rub through sieve. Add salt, milk, butter, and flour which should be blended with a little of the milk. Cook together 5 min.

Pumpkin Soup

1 T. butter, melted
2 T. onion, finely chopped
1½ c. tomatoes, cooked
1 c. pumpkin, cooked
1 c. cream
½ c. milk
1 t. salt
pepper
1 t. sugar

In melted butter saute onion until soft. Add tomatoes and pumpkin. Heat slowly. Add remaining ingredients and heat to simmering. Serve at once. Makes about 2 c.

Fish Chowder (Abe Martin Lodge)

4 T. butter
4 T. flour
4 c. milk
1 t. salt
pinch of pepper
1 c. mushrooms, sliced
1 c. mayonnaise
1/2 c. white wine
2 lb. fish fillets (lightly poached and diced)

Melt butter; stir in flour. While stirring, add milk, salt, pepper, mushrooms, and mayonnaise. Bring to a boil, add wine and fish. Let simmer 15 min. Serves 8 to 10.

Kidney Stew

1 beef kidney
1 c. potato, diced and cooked
1 T. onion, sliced thin and cooked
1 T. flour
1 T. butter, melted
1 egg yolk
1 T. parsley, chopped
2 drops Tabasco

Wash kidney, remove skin and fat. Cover with water and heat to boiling point. Drain and repeat with fresh water until no strong odor or scum is present. Add water and simmer until kidney is tender enough to cut into small pieces. Add cooked potato and onion. Thicken broth with flour blended with butter. Remove stew from heat, add egg yolk, parsley, and tobasco. Mix and serve hot.

Lamb Broth

2½ lb. lamb shoulder, cut into 4 or 5 pieces
2 t. salt
1 stalk celery
2 T. onion, chopped
1 small bay leaf
pinch of thyme

Place meat in a kettle, cover with cold water, add remaining ingredients and heat to boiling. Reduce heat and simmer 1 to 1½ hr. Cool and skim off fat. Reheat and serve with crackers.

Lamb Stew

1½ to 2 lb. lamb
bacon fat
1 clove garlic, minced
2 carrots, cut into chunks
1 turnip quartered
1 onion, chopped
1 potato, cut into chunks
salt and pepper

Cut meat into small pieces. Brown lightly in bacon fat. Add garlic at last minute; do not allow it to brown. Add carrots and water to cover. Cook slowly for 60 min. Add remaining vegetables and seasonings. Cook an additional 20 min. If stew needs thickening, add a paste of 1 T. flour diluted with water. Continue cooking and stirring for 5 min.

Beef Stew (The Ordinary)

2 lb. stew meat
water
1 beef bouillon cube
salt
pepper
garlic powder
3 lb. potatoes
1 1/2 bunches carrots
1 1/2 stalks celery
2 nice size peppers
tomato sauce

One day ahead boil the stew meat in enough water to cover meat; add water as necessary. Before meat is done, add bouillon cube, salt, pepper, and garlic powder. Refrigerate overnight for better flavor.

Peel and cut potatoes about 3/4-in. thick. Wash in cold water twice to prevent discoloring. Place in refrigerator until other vegetables are prepared. Cut celery and scraped carrots about 3/4-in. long. Cut up peppers.

Place a mixture of 1/2 water and 1/2 tomato sauce about 1-in. deep in Dutch oven. Put potatoes in pan first, next carrots and peppers, and place celery in last. Bake until almost done, add meat and bake slowly until tender. Serves 6.

Ox Tail Stew

1 ox tail
2 onions, sliced
2 T. butter
2½ qt. water
4 carrots, diced
2 turnips, diced
1 large potato, diced
1 t. Worcestershire sauce
salt and pepper
flour
1 T. parsley, chopped fine
slices of lemon

Wash the ox tail, cut in short lengths, and brown in its own fat. Cook onions in butter, add to the meat with 1½ qt. of the water and simmer until the meat is tender. In the meantime, cook the carrots and turnips for 10 min. in 1 qt. water and add to the meat with the water in which they were cooked. Add also potatoes, sauce, and salt and pepper. When the vegetables are soft, thicken the stew with a small quantity of flour mixed with a little cold water to a smooth paste. Cook until thickened. Sprinkle with parsley and slices of lemon.

Th' high cost o' food haint hurt th' ole family stew.

Pork and Parsnip Stew

1 1/4 lb. fresh pork
3 pt. hot water
3 c. parsnip, diced
1 c. onion, sliced
2 T. flour
1 T. parsley, chopped fine

Cut the pork into small pieces and brown in a skillet. Add the water and simmer the meat until nearly tender. Then add the vegetables and cook for 15 to 20 min. Mix the flour with a small quantity of cold water. Add to the meat and vegetables and cook until the stew is thickened. Add salt. Sprinkle the parsley in the stew and serve hot.

SWEET STUFF
Puddings, Pies, Cakes, Cookies, and Candy

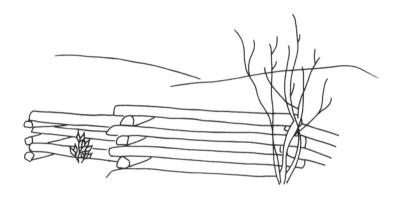

A middleman is a feller that makes a piece o' cherry pie cost twenty-five cents in spite o' th' largest cherry crop in th' world's history.

Pie Crust

$1/2$ t. salt

$1\,1/2$ c. flour, sifted

$1/2$ c. shortening

3 T. water or enough to make a stiff dough

Combine the salt, flour, and shortening, using knives or a pastry fork, until dough is mealy. Add the water slowly. Roll dough lightly. This makes a double crust.

Apple or Peach in a Poke

Roll pie pastry to a thickness of $1/8$ in. Cut into circles large enough to cover a peeled apple or peach. Place fruit in center of each pastry piece. Dot with butter and sprinkle with sugar. Crimp together the edges of each pastry poke. Moisten dough with milk, if necessary, to make sealing simple. Prick the pastries several times and place each dumpling in a buttered baking dish. Bake at 350 degrees for 45 min. or until fruit is tender and crust is light brown. Serve with a hard sauce or heavy cream.

Hard Sauce

$1/4$ c. butter

$3/4$ c. powdered sugar (or brown sugar)

$1/2$ t. vanilla

$1/2$ t. nutmeg, grated

Thoroughly cream together butter and sugar, add vanilla and nutmeg. Chill before serving.

Grape Pie

1 egg and yolk of another, beaten
1 c. sugar
1 T. flour
1 heaping c. Concord grapes, seeded
butter

Beat eggs, sugar, and flour together, then add seeded grapes. Dot with butter. Pour into unbaked pie shell. Bake at 350 degrees until firm. Beat the white of egg with a little sugar for frosting.

Green Tomato Pie

4 or 5 medium-sized green tomatoes
3/4 c. sugar
1/2 lemon, thinly sliced
1/2 t. salt
1/4 t. cinnamon
1 T. butter
1 1/2 T. cornstarch

Slice the tomatoes. Heat slowly in a saucepan with the sugar, lemon, salt, and spice until the tomatoes are tender. Add a little water if the tomatoes are not juicy. Melt the butter and combine with the cornstarch. Add this to the tomato mixture and cook until the cornstarch does not taste raw. Line a pie tin with pastry and bake this crust in a moderately hot oven until a delicate color appears. Put the tomato filling in this baked crust, moisten the edge and press the upper crust firmly over the edge of the baked lower crust. Bake about 12 min. in a hot oven, or until the upper crust is browned.

Molasses Pie

2 c. sorghum
1 c. sugar
3 eggs
1 T. butter, melted
juice of 1 lemon
pinch of nutmeg

Combine ingredients and mix well. Pour into unbaked pie shell and bake at 350 degrees until set.

Rhubarb Pie

1 c. rhubarb, chopped
1 c. white sugar
1/2 c. cold water
2 T. flour
1 T. butter
2 egg yolks, beaten

Mix rhubarb and sugar, add water and let stand 1 hr. Add remaining ingredients and mix well. Bake about 350 degrees for 45 min. When done cover with meringue made from the 2 egg whites.

Rhubarb requires lots of nerve and sugar to serve and may be taken in moderate doses three days apart til one shrinks from the very sight of it.

Squash or Pumpkin Pie

1 1/2 c. squash or pumpkin, cooked
1 c. milk
1/2 c. sugar
1 t. cinnamon
1/2 t. salt
1/2 t. allspice
1/4 t. mace
2 eggs
1 T. butter

Pour all the ingredients, except the eggs and the butter, in a double boiler. Bring to the scalding point. Beat the eggs well; add them to the hot mixture. Stir until it starts to thicken. Add the butter. Line a pie pan with pastry and bake until light brown. Pour the hot filling into the baked crust. Bake the pie in a moderately hot oven until the filling sets.

Vinegar Pie

1 c. sugar
2 eggs
2 T. cider vinegar
2 T. flour or cornstarch
1 c. water
1/2 stick butter
1 t. fresh lemon juice

Combine sugar, eggs, vinegar, flour, and water in double boiler. Stir occasionally. Cook until thick and smooth. Add butter and lemon juice at last minute. Pour into baked pie shell. Cook in 300-degree oven until filling has jelled.

Berry Cobbler

1 pt. berries
1 T. lemon juice
1/2 c. sugar
1 t. nutmeg
1 T. butter

Line deep baking dish with flaky pie crust. Fill with berries. Sprinkle with lemon juice, sugar, and nutmeg. Dot with butter. Add a top crust. Bake at 350 degrees for 35 to 40 min. Serve with cream.

Suet Pudding

2 c. dates and raisins, chopped
1 c. milk
2 eggs, beaten
2 c. bread crumbs, rolled fine
1 c. molasses
1 1/4 c. suet, chopped
1/2 t. salt
1 t. cinnamon
1 t. cloves
1 t. nutmeg
2 t. baking powder

Add milk to beaten eggs and pour over bread crumbs. Combine all other ingredients and add to bread mixture. Mix well. Pour into greased pudding mold or coffee can. Cover with lid or foil. Set on rack in kettle with about 1 in. of boiling water. Cover and steam for 3 hr. taking care that water does not boil away. Cool before serving with a hard sauce.

One idea of taking advantage of an insurance company is trying to pick cherries while standing on a chair.

Indian Pudding

5 c. milk
1/3 c. cornmeal
1/2 c. molasses
1 t. salt
1 t. ginger

Cook milk and meal in a double boiler 20 min. Add molasses, salt, and ginger; pour into a buttered pudding dish and bake for 2 hr. in a slow oven. Serve hot with cream or vanilla ice cream.

Th' feller that sticks t' grape juice 'll never need a lawyer.

Raisin Bread Pudding

4 slices raisin bread
2 c. milk, scalded
1 T. margarine
1/4 t. salt
1/2 c. sugar
2 eggs, lightly beaten
2 t. vanilla
cinnamon

Soak bread in scalded milk 5 min. Add margarine, salt, sugar, eggs, and vanilla. Pour into greased 1-qt. casserole. Dust with cinnamon. Place in pan of water. Bake in 350-degree oven for 45-50 min.

Shortcake

1 c. flour
1/2 t. salt
2 t. baking powder
3 T. sugar
3 T. butter, melted
1/2 c. milk

Sift dry ingredients together, add combined butter and milk and stir well. Bake at 450 degrees for 15 min. or until golden brown. Serve warm with berries.

Sunshine Cake

6 egg yolks
1 1/2 c. sugar
10 egg whites
pinch of salt
1 t. cream of tartar
1 c. cake flour
1/2 t. lemon extract
1/2 t. orange extract

Beat egg yolks until thick and lemon-colored. Add half the sugar and beat well. In another bowl beat whites with salt, until foaming. Add cream of tartar and beat until stiff enough to stand in soft peaks. Fold in remaining sugar. Turn yolks over whites. Gradually fold in flour and add flavorings. Bake about 1 hr., or until cake tests done, at 325 degrees in ungreased 10-in. tube pan. Cool inverted over funnel.

Soft Gingerbread

1/2 c. butter
1 c. brown sugar
3/4 c. molasses
3 eggs
3 c. flour
1 t. cinnamon
1 T. ginger
1 t. soda
1 c. sour milk

Cream butter and sugar. Add molasses, then eggs one at a time. Mix thoroughly. Sift dry ingredients and add alternately with the milk. Pour batter into 9×9-in. pan and bake in moderate 350° oven about 1 hr. or until done.

Baked Pears

Wash the pears, cut them in halves and core them. Place in a baking dish. Sprinkle with brown sugar and a little salt, dot with butter and add a very little water. Place in a moderate oven. Cover at first, until the fruit becomes soft. While the fruit is cooking, baste once or twice with the liquid in the pan.

Old-Fashioned Taffy

2 c. sugar
1 c. white syrup
1 t. butter
shaved paraffin

When sugar, syrup, and butter begin to boil, add a little shaved paraffin and let boil until it spins a thread. Flavor, cool and pull.

Peanut Brittle Puff

1/2 lb. peanut brittle
1/2 pt. heavy cream
1/4 t. vanilla
10 marshmallows

Grind the peanut brittle through the food chopper or place in a cloth and powder with a hammer. Whip the cream and then stir in the peanut brittle. Add the vanilla and marshmallows quartered. Mix well and allow to stand in the refrigerator for about 2 hr. before serving. This allows time for the marshmallows to puff and make the mixture light.

Nut Brittle

For nut brittle, use walnuts, pecans, peanuts, Brazil nuts cut in pieces, shredded coconut, or practically any other kind of nut. Puffed breakfast foods may also be used in place of nuts.

2 c. white corn syrup
2 T. vinegar
1/2 t. salt
2 c. nut kernels
2 t. vanilla

Cook the syrup, vinegar, and salt in a saucepan until a little dipped in cold water forms a soft ball. Put the nuts into this syrup, pour into an iron skillet and cook, stirring constantly, until the syrup becomes golden brown. Remove from the fire and add the vanilla. Have ready a shallow buttered pan, pour in the candy and spread it out in a thin sheet. After it is cool, remove from the pan and crack into pieces.

VARIOUS
VEGETABLES

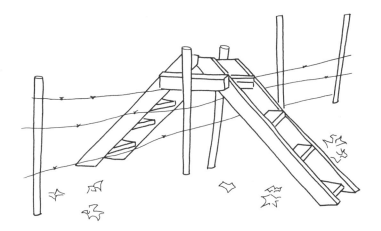

*Next to separating the goats
from the sheep, the hardest thing is
separating peas from chopped
carrots.*

Scalloped Asparagus

1 lb. fresh asparagus
5 eggs, hard boiled
2 c. macaroni, boiled
2 c. cream sauce
1/2 c. bread crumbs, buttered
1 c. cheese, grated

In a buttered casserole place layers of asparagus, chopped egg, macaroni, and cream sauce. Spread crumbs and cheese over all. Bake 1/2 hr.

Cream Sauce

Add 4 T. flour to 4 T. melted butter. Stir in 2 c. milk. Boil until thick. Season with salt and pepper.

Green Beans

Wash and prepare beans. Place 1/4 c. bacon fat in heavy vessel and, when hot, add beans and stir constantly for 10 min. over hot fire. Add 3/4 c. water (to 2 qt. prepared beans) and place on lid, having fire at its lowest. Do not lift lid for 1 hr. or more. Add salt and serve.

> *Say what you please about home, it's the only place in the world where they seem to know how to cook string beans.*

Baked Corn

4 ears corn
1/2 c. bread crumbs
1/2 t. salt
1 t. sugar
2 eggs
1/2 c. milk
butter

Cut the corn off the cob. Mix corn, bread crumbs, salt, and sugar. Beat eggs until very light. Stir in milk and add to corn mixture. Turn into well-buttered baking dish. Dot with bits of butter and bake 40 min. at 350 degrees.

A pug nose comes in mighty handy during the roasting ear season.

Corn Oysters

1 pt. sweet corn, grated
1 egg
1/2 c. cream
1/2 t. baking powder
1 cup flour
salt and pepper

Mix and bake on griddle like pancakes. Serve with crisp bacon.

Five-Minute Cabbage

1 qt. cabbage, shredded fine
1 pt. milk
2 T. butter
2 T. flour
1 c. milk
salt and pepper

Boil cabbage and milk together for 2 min. Melt butter, add flour and blend together. Add milk gradually and cook until smooth. Season with salt and pepper. Add the cabbage and milk mixture and cook, stirring for 3 min. Can be put into casserole and covered with buttered crumbs. Brown.

Baked Cucumbers

3 good-sized cucumbers
3/4 c. fine bread crumbs
3 T. butter
1/2 t. salt
1 1/2 T. onion, chopped
1 1/2 t. parsley, finely chopped
3 t. celery, chopped
1 c. tomatoes, cut in pieces

Wash cucumbers and cut in half lengthwise. Scoop out as much as possible of the pulp without breaking the skin. Brown the onion in the fat. Add other ingredients mixed with the cucumber pulp. Stir constantly and cook 5 min. or until dry. Place filling in cucumber shells and bake until the shells are soft and the mixture is brown on top.

Panned Kale

Strip the kale from the midribs. Discard ribs and stringy portions. Wash kale thoroughly in several changes of water and cut into small pieces. For each qt. of kale allow 2 T. butter or other fat. Melt the fat in a skillet, add the kale and cover the skillet to keep in the steam, which forms when the juices of the kale are drawn out by the heat. The kale will be done in from 10 to 20 min. Sift 1 t. of flour over the greens. Mix well, pour in 1/2 c. milk and stir until thickened. Season with salt and pepper.

Baked Lima Beans

2 c. limas, cooked
1 c. bacon, diced
2 T. onion, chopped
4 T. green pepper, chopped
4 T. brown sugar
2 c. tomato juice
1 t. salt
1/3 c. cheese, grated
1 c. bread crumbs

Soak dried beans overnight. Cook until tender and drain. Brown bacon, remove and crumble. Add onion and pepper to drippings and cook until tender. Add remaining ingredients and simmer 10 min. Pour into oven-proof dish and top with grated cheese and crumbs. Bake at 350 degrees for 40 min.

Scalloped Parsnips

6 or 7 medium parsnips
3 T. butter
2 T. flour
1/2 c. parsnip water
1/2 c. rich milk
buttered bread crumbs

Scrub parsnips clean. Cook until tender in lightly salted water 20 to 30 minutes. Drain and scrape off outer skin. Split the parsnips lengthwise. Pull out the woody cores. Place the parsnips in a shallow baking dish. Cover them with a white sauce made with the butter, flour, parsnip water, and milk. Cover top with bread crumbs which have been mixed with melted butter. Bake in a moderate oven until the parsnips are thoroughly heated and the buttered crumbs are golden grown.

Scalloped Rhubarb

4 T. butter
3 c. bread crumbs
2 c. rhubarb, cut in small pieces
1/2 c. sugar
1/2 c. seedless raisins

Melt butter and add to crumbs. Put layer in baking dish, then rhubarb, sugar, and raisins. Repeat and cover with crumbs. Bake in slow oven about 1 hr. and serve warm with meat course.

Rhubarb bores through the ground real early in March – and it's appearance is never postponed on account of weather.

Peanuts and Scalloped Onions

4 to 6 medium-sized onions
$1/2$ to $3/4$ c. peanuts, ground
1 c. thin cream sauce, made with
1 T. flour, 1 T. butter and 1 c. milk

Cook skinned onions in boiling water until tender. Drain and slice with a sharp knife. In a greased baking dish, place the onions in layers with the peanuts and cream sauce until all ingredients are used. Cover the top with buttered crumbs and bake in a moderate oven until golden brown. Serve from the baking dish.

It's claimed that onions are good fer th' nerves an' we've often noticed th' two t'gether.

Potato Dumplings

1 c. flour
1 t. baking powder
$1/4$ t. salt
$1/2$ c. milk
1 egg, beaten
1 c. potatoes, mashed
1 qt. broth

Sift dry ingredients together. Add milk, beaten egg, and mashed potatoes. Mix lightly until smooth. Wet spoon in 1 qt. boiling hot broth in deep saucepan. Drop by rounded spoonfuls into the broth, wetting spoon each time. Cover partially and boil gently until all are done when gently pricked with a fork.

There's no appeal fer a left o'er baked p'tater.

Spinach

1 lb. spinach
2 T. butter
1 T. onion, chopped
1 c. ham, diced
2 T. bread crumbs
1/2 t. salt
1/8 t. pepper
pinch of nutmeg
1 c. soup stock

Pick off the roots and decayed leaves. Wash in 3 or 4 changes of water. Put the spinach in a large kettle without water. Let cook slowly until some of the juice is drawn out, then boil about 15 min. or until tender. Drain thoroughly and cut very fine. Heat the butter, add onion, ham, bread crumbs, seasonings, and gradually the soup stock. Stir in spinach. Heat through. If desired, garnish with poached or hard-boiled eggs, sliced.

> *Wouldn' it be awful if spinach hain't really health-*
> *ful after all th' trouble it takes t' git th' sand out*
> *of it?*

Baked Tomatoes and Eggs

Tomatoes
Salt
Eggs
Butter

Select smooth, good-sized tomatoes. Cut out the stem. Scoop out part of the meat of the tomatoes, being careful not to break the skin. Sprinkle with salt, break an egg into the tomato cup, add a lump of butter, put into a buttered pan with just enough water to keep from scorching, and bake in a moderate oven 5 to 10 min. or until eggs are done.

Turnip or Carrot Custard

2 eggs
1/2 t. salt
1 c. raw turnip, grated or cooked turnip, mashed
1 pt. milk
few drops Tabasco
2 T. melted butter

Beat eggs lightly. Add salt, turnip, milk, and tabasco. Stir in melted butter and bake in a moderate oven in a pan surrounded by water, until custard is set in the center. Serve at once. Carrots may be used in the same way as turnips.

It don't look very good fer th' steady revival o' business t' see th' newspapers filled with recipes for creamed carrots.

Casserole of Vegetables

1 c. lima beans
2 c. celery, diced
1/2 c. green pepper, minced
4 medium-sized onions, sliced
2 c. canned tomatoes
salt and pepper
2 T. butter or bacon slices

Wash beans and soak overnight in water to cover. Cook until tender. Drain off surplus water and add celery, green pepper, onions, tomatoes, salt and pepper. Top with bacon or dot with butter. Bake at 350 degrees in buttered casserole for 1 hr.

Hopping John

1/2 c. dried black-eyed peas
1/4 lb. salt pork or bacon, diced
1/2 c. rice, cooked
salt and pepper

Bring peas to a boil in 3 c. water and cook for 2 min. Cover and soak for 1 hr. Add pork. Simmer until peas are tender. Season to taste. Serve with rice.

Salsify (oyster plant)

salsify roots
butter or margarine
salt

Prepare roots by scrubbing and peeling or scraping. Boil for 30 min. in salted water. Serve like buttered carrots or parsnips.

Sweet Potato Balls

Boil sweet potatoes with a little salt. Mash and roll in a ball around a marshmallow. Roll in cornflake crumbs and fry in fat until heated through.

SOMETHING WILD
IN THE KITCHEN

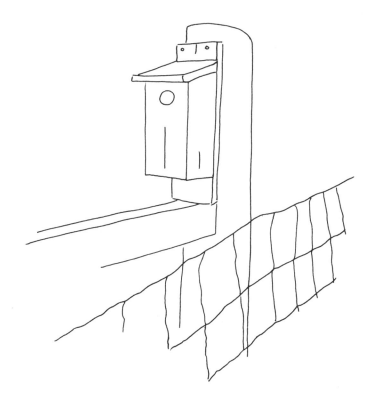

Farming looks nice from a car window.

Baked Carp

In dressing do not remove skin from fish, but scrape and wash thoroughly, then place in flour sack.

Parboil in salt water with onions and celery about 1 hr. Remove from water, take out of flour sack, dry, stuff with celery leaves, rub with salt and pepper. Place in large pan and bake about 1/2 hr. Arrange on platter garnished with cooked vegetables. Serve with lemon sauce.

Bluegill Chowder

8 oz. fish, flaked
4 strips bacon
1 medium onion, diced
1 c. potatoes, diced
1 c. celery, diced
1 c. carrots, diced
flour
4 c. milk
salt and pepper

Clean and scale fish. Poach, in water to cover, for several min. until skin loosens. Remove skin and bones and set flaked flesh aside. Brown bacon and saute onion until soft but not brown. Drain bacon, crumble, and transfer it with onion to a soup pot. Add vegetables and water to cover. Simmer until tender. Add flour to thicken. Pour in milk and heat slowly to prevent scalding. When mixture is heated through, add flaked fish. Allow fish to heat, but not cook. Ladle into bowls and add a pat of butter to surface of chowder.

Fried Fish

fresh caught fish
evaporated milk
cracker crumbs
hot fat

Dip cleaned and scaled fish, whole or filleted, into milk and roll in crumbs. In a heavy iron skillet, heat fat just short of smoking. Do not let fat get too hot. Fry each fish piece, turning once. Fish is done as soon as it flakes.

Wild Stew

4 qt. water
1 1/2 to 2 lb. rabbit, squirrel or woodchuck
1 chicken
1 c. onions, chopped
5 green peppers, chopped
2 T. bacon drippings
2 cans 16-ounce tomatoes
1 can lima beans
1 c. carrots, diced
2 c. potatoes, diced
2 bay leaves
2 cans corn
1/4 t. thyme
salt and pepper

Place all disjointed, parboiled meat in large pot of water. Bring to boil, add disjointed chicken, reduce heat and simmer for 1 1/2 hr. or until all meat and chicken is removed easily from the bones. Saute onions and green peppers in bacon drippings. Add these and all other ingredients to the stew pot. Simmer mixture for 45 to 60 min. or until vegetables are done. Correct seasoning. Serves 8.

Roast Venison

6 or 7 lb. saddle or leg roast
1/4 c. vinegar
1/2 c. water
flour
garlic salt
currant jelly (optional)

Mix vinegar and water. Wipe meat with this diluted mixture. Set oven for 450 degrees. Roast at this temperature for 1/2 hr. Dredge roast with flour and garlic salt. Reduce heat to 350 degrees and continue roasting until meat is done. Total cooking time equals 20 min. per lb. Once flour has browned, glaze roast with currant jelly, if desired. Add water to roasting pan to keep juices from sticking. Baste frequently.

Next to being mistaken for a wealthy widow, the most dangerous thing is looking like a deer.

Baked Rabbit

1 rabbit
3 c. cream or a thin white sauce
6 slices bacon
flour

Skin, clean, and wash the rabbit. Split into 2 pieces cutting along the backbone. Rub with salt and a little pepper. Place in a roasting pan. Dredge with flour. Lay strips of bacon across the rabbit. Pour over and around it 3 c. of white sauce or 3 c. of cream. Bake 1 1/2 hr., basting frequently, at 325 degrees. Serve hot with cream gravy. The liver may be boiled until tender, chopped and added to the gravy before serving.

Dressing Quail for Broiling

Singe, wipe, and with a sharp pointed knife beginning at back of neck, make a cut through backbone the entire length of bird. Lay open the bird and remove contents from inside. Cut out rib bones on either side of backbone, remove from breastbone, then cut through tendons at joints. Chicken is prepared in the same manner for broiling.

Broiled Quail

Dress for broiling. Sprinkle with salt and pepper and place in a well-greased broiler. Broil 8 to 10 min. turning pieces so that all parts may be equally browned. Serve on toast, garnish with parsley and thin slices of lemon. Currant jelly is nice served with this course.

Fried Quail

8 cleaned birds
salt and pepper
1 c. flour
oil or bacon drippings
$^1/_2$ c. water
$^1/_4$ c. flour
2 c. milk

Season birds and dredge in flour. Heat oil or drippings in an iron skillet. Fry birds until golden brown. Turn each piece at least once. Remove birds and set aside. Reserve only $^1/_2$ c. grease in skillet. Add water and quail. Cover and simmer for 15 to 20 min. Remove tender birds. In remaining drippings, add $^1/_4$ c. flour and stir and simmer until gravy is smooth. Add milk gradually, season to taste, and serve hot gravy with fried birds.

Fried Frogs

Contrary to usual supposition, the front legs and backs of frogs can be eaten as well as the hind legs. Clean, salt, and cut tendons in legs to keep from "hopping," dip in flour, mixed lightly with pepper, fry in hot fat in covered skillet, until brown.

Hot, Roasted Chestnuts

Cut an X into the flat side of each nut. Place nuts in roasting pan and bake at 400 degrees for 20 to 25 min. Allow to cool, but peel and eat while still warm.

Wild Chicory Coffee

Chicory roots should be dug as soon as plant stops blooming. Scrub roots and dry whole in moderate oven. When roasted roots turn a dark brown, cool and grind into coffee.

Brew chicory coffee. Add an equal amount of hot milk and maybe a pinch or two of ground cinnamon.

Clover Tea

Collect red clover blossoms while in full bloom. Spread flat on a window screen until thoroughly dried. Store in airtight jars.

Steep dried blooms in boiling water. Serve with sugar and lemon to taste.

Drinking from a saucer will wrinkle the forehead.

Dandelion Greens, Wilted

2 qt. dandelion greens
4 T. bacon fat
1/4 cup mild vinegar
1 t. salt

Wash the greens thoroughly. Cut finely with scissors. Place the greens in a skillet and add the bacon fat, vinegar, and salt. Cover until the greens are wilted and then serve at once.

Dandelion Jelly

1 qt. dandelion blossoms
1 qt. water
1 pkg. pectin
2 T. lemon juice
4 1/2 c. sugar
yellow food coloring

Rinse the blossoms carefully. Boil them in the water for 3 min.; strain out 3 of the c. of water. Return to stove and add lemon juice and pectin. When this begins to boil, add sugar and boil 3 min. Pour into jars and seal. This jelly tastes like honey. Food coloring is optional, but makes it an attractive color.

Rose Hip Jam

1 lb. rose hips
1 c. water
1 lb. sugar

In an enamel pan, cook rose hips in water until the fruit is soft. Force pulp through a ricer or colander. Return pulp to pan, add sugar and cook over low heat until mixture is thick. Pour into jelly glasses and seal.

Baked Paw Paws

paw paws
confectioner's sugar
lemon juice

Prick skins of fruit with a fork. Place paw paws in a buttered baking dish and bake at 350 degrees until tender. Split open baked fruit and serve with powdered sugar and lemon juice.

Paw Paw Pie

1 1/2 c. peeled and diced paw paws
1 c. sugar
1 c. milk
1 egg
1/4 t. salt

Combine ingredients and cook over moderate heat until thickened. Pour mixture into unbaked pie shell and bake at 350 degrees until crust is done.

Persimmon Butter

8 c. persimmon pulp
4 t. baking soda
4 c. sugar
juice of 1 lemon
grated rind of 1 lemon
2 t. allspice

Wash persimmons, stem, and remove seeds. Heat pulp in double boiler until soft. Press through a food mill. Add remaining ingredients. Heat and stir frequently until thick. Pour into hot jars and seal. Process 10 min. in hot water bath. Makes 5 pt.

Pine Needle Tea

Gather several handfuls of green needles from lower branches of a white pine tree. Use scissors to cut needles into small pieces and steep them in boiling water for 10 to 15 min. Serve with sugar or honey.

Poke Sprouts

Wash and trim young shoots, place in shallow pan and cover with water. Bring to boil, reduce heat, simmer for 10 min. Drain, cover with fresh water and cook again for 20 or more min. until poke is tender, like asparagus. Season with salt and pepper and add butter or cream sauce.

Puffballs in Foil

puffballs, sliced
olive oil or butter
salt and pepper
garlic powder (use conservatively)

Clean, parboil, and slice enough puffballs for the number of servings you need. Dip the mushroom slices in oil or melted butter. Arrange one layer of slices on large pieces of heavy duty aluminum foil and sprinkle with seasonings. Bring the ends of the foil together and seal tightly. Puffballs may be cooked in a 350-degree oven for about 20 min. or on a charcoal grill long enough to heat through.

Mint Sauce

Run well-washed, fresh mint, rid of large stems, through food chopper. Add 1 T. hot water and let stand a few minutes. Add pinch of salt and 1 T. sugar and clear vinegar making rather thin sauce. Serve cold with hot lamb.

Fried Mushrooms (Morels)

Soak morels in salt water to get rid of insects. Pat dry and dip in an egg batter. Fry in drippings or oil ¼ to ½ in. deep.

Nettle Soup

nettle leaves
chicken broth or stock
barley or rice
seasoning

For each qt. of nettle leaves, prepare 5 c. of broth or stock. Add ¼ c. barley or rice. Bring soup to boil and simmer for 30 min. or more. Season to taste. Serve hot.

Mayapple Wild Lemon Marmalade

½ gal. of fresh, ripe Mayapples
1 c. water
1 3-oz. pkg. powdered pectin
5 c. sugar
food coloring, if desired

Wash the fruit and remove stem and blossom ends. Cut the Mayapples in halves or quarters, depending on size. Add water and simmer mixture in a large kettle until the fruit is very soft and juicy. Fifteen min. of cooking with frequent stirring to prevent sticking should be sufficient. Using a food mill or ricer, extract juice and pulp, leaving skins and seeds as residue. Return pulp and juice to kettle and add pectin. Bring to a boil and add sugar. Stirring constantly, allow mixture to reach and maintain a rolling boil for 1 full min. Ladle into ½-pt. jelly glasses and seal appropriately.

Sassafras Candy

2 c. sugar
1 c. strong sassafras tea

Heat sugar until melted. Add tea and mix thoroughly until sugar is completely dissolved. Pour candy on flat surface to cool. Break into pieces and enjoy delicious "root-beer" flavored candy.

Sassafras Jelly

4 c. sassafras tea
5 c. sugar
3/4 t. citric acid or sour salt
1 pkg. dry pectin

Brew strong tea. Add sugar and citric acid, stir until boiling point is reached. Add pectin and continue to boil, stirring constantly until jelly forms in drops on tip of raised spoon. Ladle into sterilized glasses and seal with parafin.

Sassafras Tea

Dig sassafras root in the spring when it is easy to pull up. Scrub roots and cut into small pieces. Dry surplus roots and store in airtight jar.

For tea, heat a kettle of water and steep a handful of roots, boil until tea turns a rich, red color. Sweeten with sugar or honey.

Black Walnut Waffles

3/4 c. walnuts, chopped
2 c. flour
2 t. baking powder
1/2 t. baking soda
3/4 t. salt
3 eggs
1 c. sour cream
1/2 c. butter
1 c. milk

Sift flour, baking powder, soda, and salt together. Separate eggs and beat the yolks until they are a light lemon color. Mix yolks with sour cream. Melt butter and add it to the flour mixture along with eggs and sour cream. Slowly add milk, stirring constantly. Add nuts and mix thoroughly. Beat egg whites until small peaks indicate stiffness. Fold egg whites into mixture. Pour batter onto waffle iron and cook to desired crispness. Serve with syrup or jelly.

Black Walnut Refrigerator Cookies

3 1/2 c. flour, sifted
1/4 t. salt
1 t. baking soda
2 c. brown sugar
1 c. butter
2 eggs
1 c. black walnuts

Combine flour, salt, and soda. Cream sugar and butter. Beat eggs and add to creamed mixture. Blend in dry ingredients; add nuts. Shape dough into a long roll, wrap and refrigerate. Slice roll into rounds 1/8-in. thick. Bake cookies for 8 min. in preheated 350-degree oven.

Black Walnut Chocolate Fudge

3 T. butter, melted
1/2 c. cocoa
2 1/2 c. granulated sugar
pinch of salt
1/2 c. top milk or sour cream
vanilla to taste
1 c. nuts, chopped

Stir first 5 ingredients together and bring to a slow boil. Boil until forms a soft ball in cold water. Add vanilla and let cool 15 min. Add nutmeats and beat until creamy. Pour out on well-buttered pan.

The boy that got his fingers stained hulling walnuts now has a daughter that smokes cigarettes.

Black Walnut Pie

2 egg yolks, beaten
1 c. sugar
2 T. flour
2 T. butter
1 c. milk
1 c. walnuts, chopped
2 egg whites, stiffly beaten

Cook egg yolks, 1/2 c. sugar, flour, butter, and milk together until thick enough for pie. Add walnuts and cool. Add 1/2 c. sugar to the stiffly beaten egg whites. Fold into nut mixture and pour into baked pastry shell. Chill for several hrs. Top with whipped cream.

Blackberry Flummery

2 c. blackberry juice
1/2 c. sugar
3 T. farina or cornstarch
1/4 t. salt
2 t. lemon juice

Heat the blackberry juice. Mix sugar, farina or cornstarch, salt, and add to juice. Heat mixture in double boiler until it thickens. Remove from heat, add lemon juice and beat energetically. Flummery should be served cold with whipped cream.

(Delicious) Nut Bread

3 c. flour
1 c. sugar
2 T. baking powder
1 t. salt
1 c. hickory nuts, chopped
1 egg, beaten lightly
1 c. sweet milk

Sift together dry ingredients. Add nuts, then the beaten egg with the milk. Mix to a dough. Turn into a well-greased loaf pan, let stand 15 min. and bake 45 min. at 350 degrees.

A woman might bake bread but wasn't supposed to win any.

Persimmon Pudding (Abe Martin Lodge)

2 c. flour
2 c. sugar
2 t. baking powder
2 c. milk
2 eggs, slightly beaten
2 c. persimmon pulp
2 t. vanilla
1 t. soda dissolved in 1/4 c. hot water

Mix flour, sugar, and baking powder in a large bowl. Add milk a little at a time until smooth. Stir in remaining ingredients. Pour into ungreased 9×13-in. pan. Bake at 350 degrees about 1 hr. or until uniformly dark.

Snow Ice Cream

1 can evaporated milk
2 T. sugar
1/8 t. salt
flavoring (vanilla, cocoa, peppermint)
clean, fresh snow

Place milk and seasonings in a large bowl. Quickly add snow to taste.

Elderberry Wine

4 lb. berries, stemmed
1 gal. water
3 1/2 lb. white sugar
1 pkg. all-purpose wine yeast
1/2 oz. citric acid

Mash berries in a crock.. Add boiling water. Stir well and cover. Allow mixture to rest for 5 to 7 days. Stir occasionally to keep berries submerged. Strain juice and combine with sugar, yeast, and citric acid. Pour wine into a large covered container until fermentation is complete (bubbling stops). Siphon off into dark bottles. Allow wine to age for several months (at least).

Elderberry wine will not age in a glass.

COUNTRY
WISDOM

Abe Martin says:

"Lemon juice'll clean elbows."

Cooking

Green beans, turnips, and potatoes will have a more natural flavor if cooked unsalted. Use butter as a sauce and salt before serving.

A teaspoon of salt may equal a cupful of sugar in counteracting sourness in berries.

Tea should never be steeped in a metal pot. Always use a china, glass, or pottery teapot.

Clamp teeth tightly on a wooden matchstick when peeling onions. Tears will not form.

To prevent nuts and fruits from sinking in cakes, heat before dusting with flour and adding to cake batter.

Add one teaspoon baking powder to strong flavored vegetables such as cabbage and cauliflower. Odor will be less noticeable.

Tea must always be put "to draw" never to boil. Then let it steep for at least three minutes.

To peel a fresh tomato easily, hold it over a gas flame for a few seconds to split the skin.

Add three-fourths cup crushed ginger snaps to liquid for a good brown gravy.

Sprinkle fresh buttered popcorn on thick, hot soup just before serving.

Housekeeping

Tea or coffee stains can be removed from marble table tops with full strength ammonia.

Put a hedge apple (osage orange) under the sink to keep roaches away.

Remove smoke stains from fireplace brick and stone by scrubbing with straight vinegar.

A mixture of one pint kerosene to a bucket of water will make windows shine.

Polish antique furniture with a mixture of six ounces linseed oil, six ounces turpentine, and six ounces vinegar.

Wrap your silver serving pieces in large pieces of waxed paper and they will not tarnish. Twist ends of paper so no air can enter.

To remove mildew from shoes and boots wipe with a half-and-half water-alcohol mixture and then apply polish or wax.

Red ants can be driven away with a generous sprinkling of powdered cinnamon.

That old copper wash boiler will clean up fine if you use one teaspoon salt mixed with the juice of one lemon and scrub with 4.0 steel wool. Rinse boiler with water and apply a paste wax to preserve shine.

Erase water marks on fine furniture by rubbing with a mixture of butter and cigarette ashes.

Home Maintenance

Sprinkle lime on a shake roof to keep it clear of moss.

Sprinkle talcum powder between floor boards to kill the squeak.

To free a stuck glass bottle stopper, mix some alcohol with a small amount of glycerin and table salt. Soak stopper for a day or so and then tap it to jar it loose.

As soon as the sun sets, draw all shades in the house to conserve heat.

A can of leftover paint will keep longer if it is stored upside down.

To mend cracks in a cast-iron stove, mix a pint of wood ashes with three teaspoons salt, and enough water to make a paste. Fill cracks while the stove is hot.

Sagging cane chair seats and backs can be tightened by placing a wet towel over the sagging area for an hour or so. Remove the towel and place chair in hot sun until cane tightens.

Keep wicker furniture dusted and oiled to prevent cracking and splitting. Use lemon oil and don't forget to use it on the under surfaces as well.

Buy a small piece of camphor from your druggist and put it in the tool box to prevent rust.

Use sandpaper to smooth burnt pans, griddles, skillets, and kettles, both inside and out.

Index